NATIONAL
GEOGRAPHIC

What Can a Diver See?

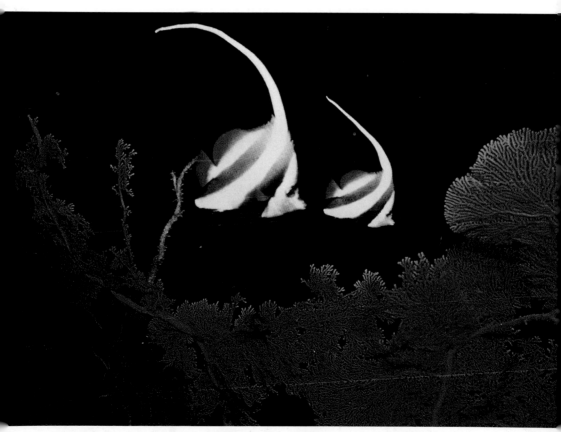

Jacob Fink

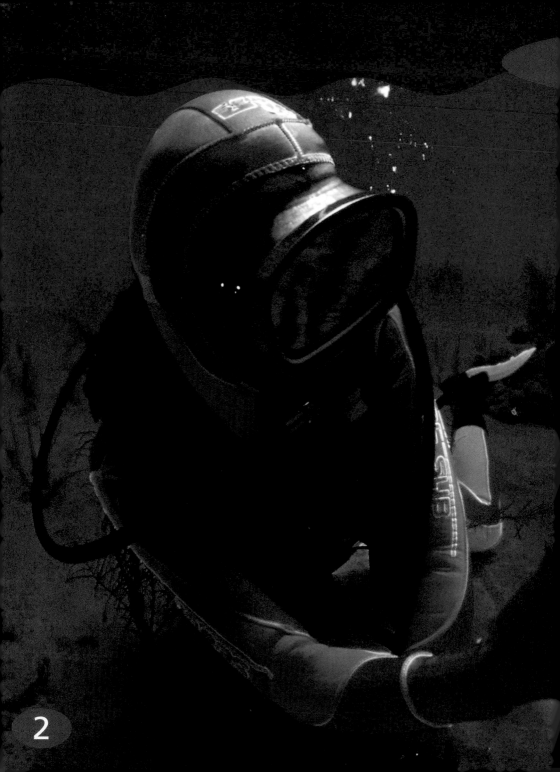

What can a diver see?

What can a diver see?

starfish

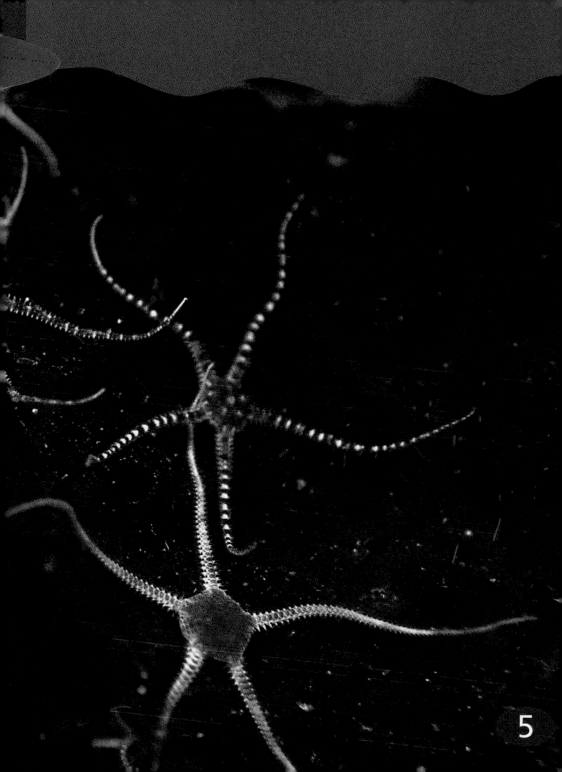

5

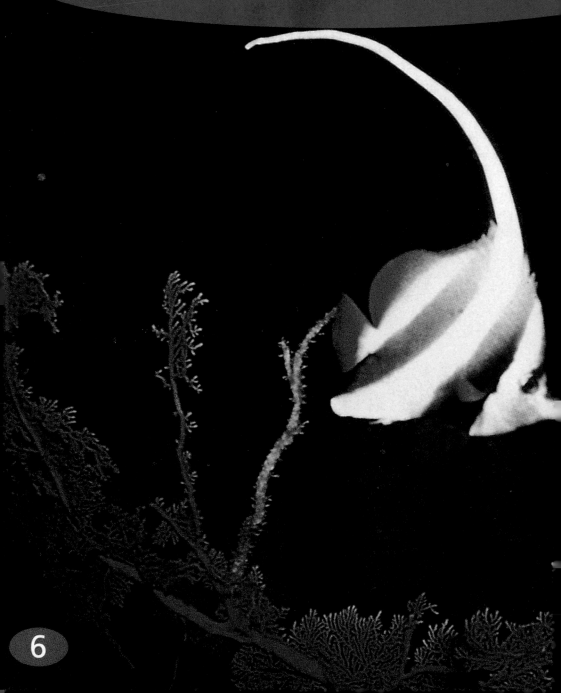

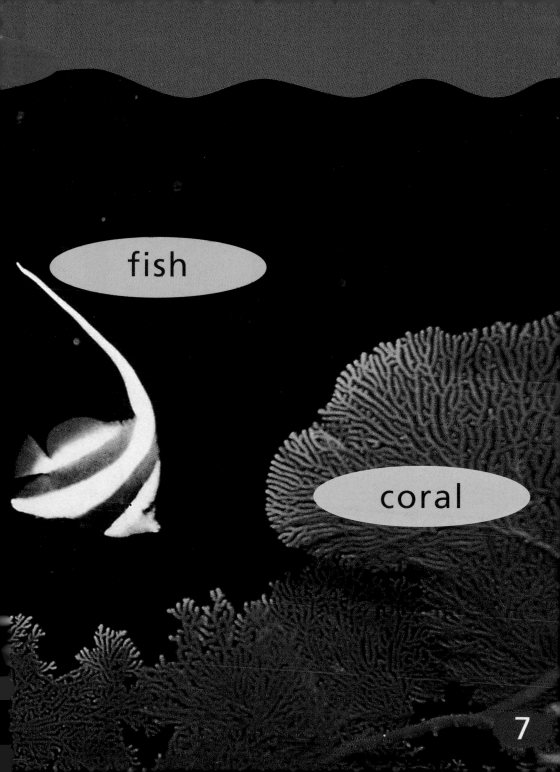

fish

coral

What can a diver see?

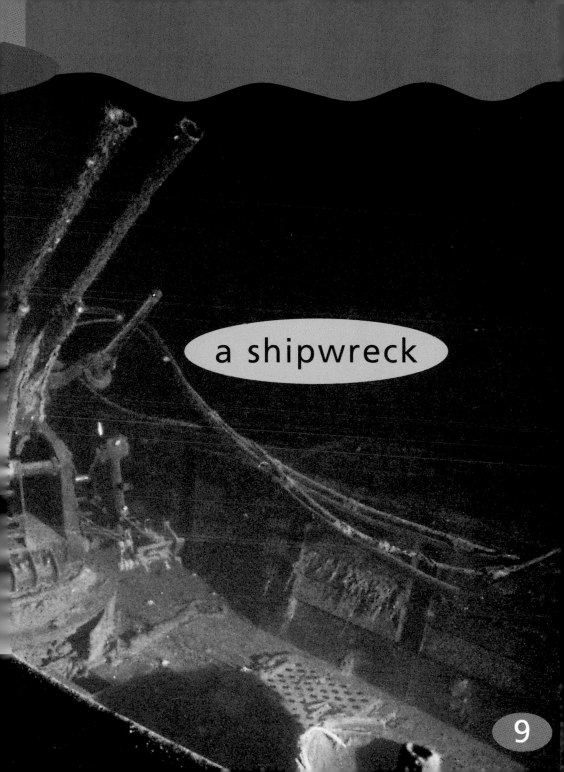

a shipwreck

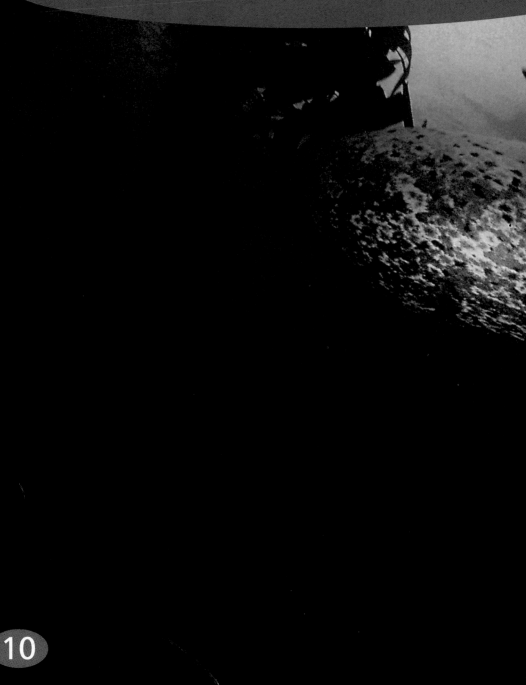

What can a diver see?

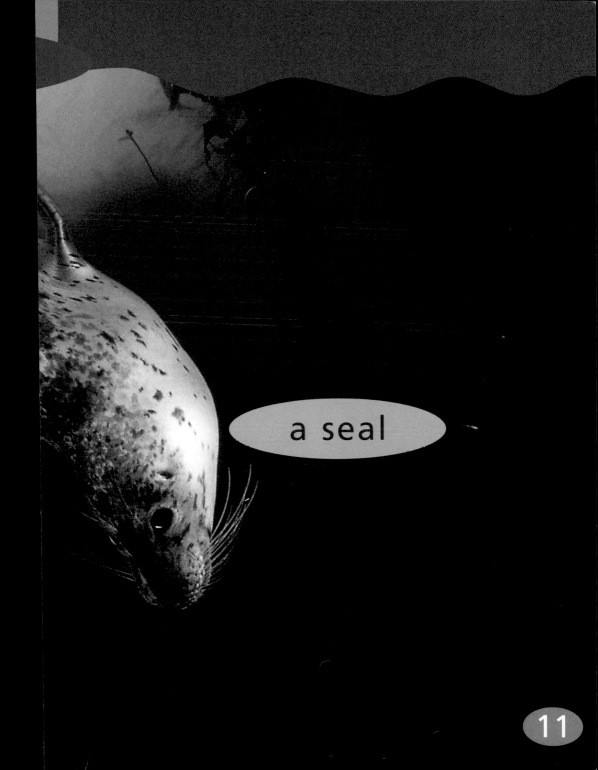

a seal

What can a diver see?

another diver!